African Safari & Painted Moments

ADULT COLORING BOOK WITH POETRY AND SELF-DISCOVERY

Aventuras De Viaje

Copyright SF Nonfiction Books © 2024

All Rights Reserved

No part of this document may be reproduced without written consent from the author.

www.SFNonfictionBooks.com

INTRODUCTION

Welcome to a world where the wild roams free, where the majestic beauty of the African safari intertwines with the enchanting world of colors. This isn't just any coloring book—it's an expedition, a retreat, and a celebration of the diverse and captivating wildlife of Africa.

Each page brings you closer to the heart of the savannah, where lions, elephants, giraffes, and many more roam under the vast, open skies. These animals, symbols of strength, grace, and the untamed spirit of nature, are waiting to be brought to life with your vibrant palette. Coloring these creatures is not only a creative journey but also a way to connect with the raw beauty of the African wilderness.

In our fast-paced lives, taking a moment for ourselves is vital. Coloring provides a chance to slow down, to be present, and to rekindle our relationship with the natural world. It's an opportunity to unleash that childlike sense of wonder and let it shine through in a spectrum of colors.

Embrace this artistic safari, immersing yourself in the African landscape and the therapeutic act of coloring. Here, you're not just exploring a continent; you're rediscovering the joys of creativity and the peace of mindfulness.

Discovering the Mosaic of Imagination

Dive deeper, and you'll find that this book has been meticulously crafted to enhance your personal journey:

- **Simple Activities:** Beyond just coloring, engage with activities designed to spark reflection and creativity. These gentle prompts will lead you to moments of introspection, serving as kindling for your inner fire.

- **Quotes:** Let the wisdom of personal development accompany you, illuminating your path as you add your own burst of color to the pages.

- **Positive Affirmations:** As you color, let these words of positivity uplift your spirit, molding your thoughts and inspiring a brighter perspective.

- **Poems and Haikus**: Delight in the poetic tales that complement the theme of this book, capturing life's varied rhythms and experiences. Each verse and every line serve as a muse for your artistic endeavors, enhancing your coloring journey with lyrical inspiration.

Embark on this coloring odyssey, immersing yourself in a world of diverse themes and the therapeutic embrace of art. Each page invites you on a unique journey, blending your creativity with the tranquility of coloring.

THANKS FOR YOUR PURCHASE

Get Your Next SF Nonfiction Book FREE!

Claim the book of your choice at:

www.SFNonfictionBooks.com/Free-Book

You will also be among the first to know of all the latest releases, discount offers, bonus content, and more.

Go to:

www.SFNonfictionBooks.com/Free-Book

Thanks again for your support.

Nature's Beauty:
Share your favorite sight from the safari.

_____

_____

"Embrace the wild within to discover your true self."

I embrace the adventure of life like a fearless explorer.

In the heart of Africa's embrace, A wild adventure, a sacred space. Lions roar, eagles soar, A journey like none before.

Acts of Kindness:
Describe a kind act you witnessed or did today.

_____

_____

"In the heart of the wilderness, find the essence of your soul."

I find strength and courage in the heart of the wilderness.

Savannah's sunrise, Lions roam as day awakes, Nature's heart alive.

Gratitude Journal:
List three things you're grateful for right now.

_____

_____

"Life is an adventure; make your journey a safari of the soul."

I am one with the beauty and diversity of the safari.

Serengeti's vast plains extend, Where life and beauty know no end. Under the African sky so wide, In this wild realm, we take a ride.

Wildlife Wisdom:
Reflect on a life lesson inspired by safari animals.

_____

_____

"Strength comes from facing the unknown with courage."

I see the extraordinary in the ordinary moments of life.

Elephants so grand, Beneath the African sky, In their world we stand.

African Adventure:
Share your dream safari destination.

_____

_____

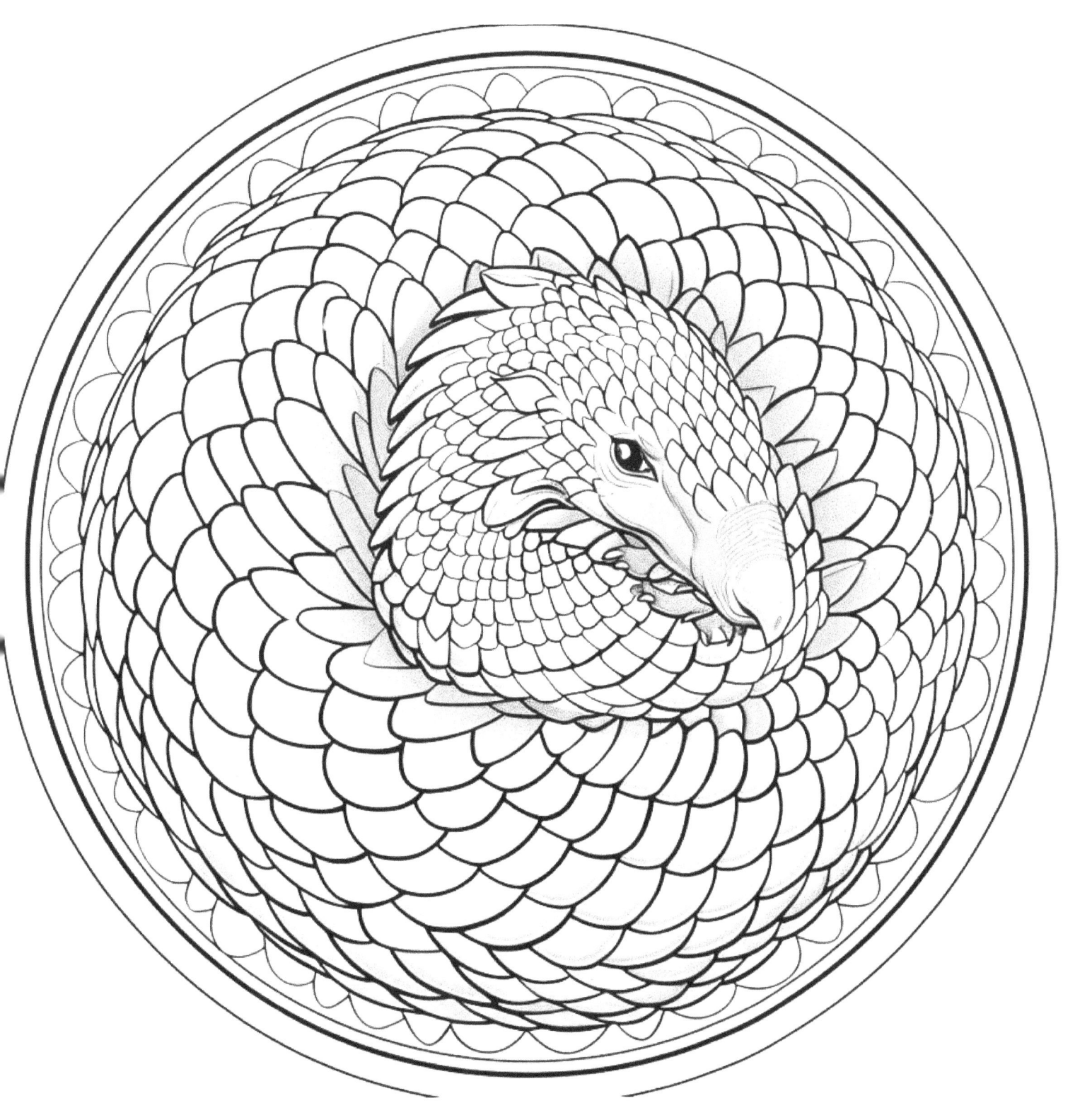

"Just as animals adapt, so can we in the face of change."

I am adaptable and resilient, just like the savanna.

Safari's call, a thrilling quest,
Nature's beauty at its best.
Elephants, zebras, and giraffes so tall, A tapestry of life, a wonder for all.

Roar of Positivity:
How can you spread positivity today?

_____

_____

"In the wild, patience and perseverance lead to greatness."

I thrive in the wild unknown, where my potential is limitless.

Zebras in a line, Stripes in black and white so bold, Nature's design shines.

Safari Serenity:
Write about a peaceful moment in nature.

_____

_____

"Like a safari, life's beauty lies in its diversity."

I release what no longer serves me, like the setting sun.

In the land where lions play, We find our path, a wild array. From sunrise to sunset, the savanna's grace, In this enchanting realm, we find our place.

Conservation Commitment: Pledge to protect wildlife and their habitats.

_____

_____

"As the sun sets, let go of what no longer serves you."

I am patient and persistent, like nature's cycles.

Sunset's golden glow, Silhouettes on the landscape, Day to night, we flow.

Safari Reflection:
What does the safari teach you about life?

_____

_____

"Survival is about adaptability and resilience."

I radiate positivity and kindness,
like the African sun.

African dreams in colors untold, In every step, a story unfolds. From morning's light to twilight's hue, The wild safari, a dream come true.

Kindness Begets Kindness:
Share a recent act of kindness you experienced.

_____

_____

"The greatest adventures begin outside your comfort zone."

I cherish the journey of life, just as
I cherish a safari.

Giraffe's graceful stride, Reaching for the treetop's crown, Nature's artistry.

Sunset Solace:
Describe the tranquility of a safari sunset.

_____

_____

"Like the safari, life is a journey to cherish."

I find wisdom in the whispers of the natural world.

Serengeti's plains, Stretching to the horizon, Life's wild domains.

African Dreams:
Write down a dream you have for Africa's future.

_____

_____

"Growth occurs when you step into the wild unknown."

I am on a path of discovery, just like an African explorer.

On the horizon where sky meets land, A journey of discovery, so grand. With every step, we write our story, In the wild's embrace, we find our glory.

Safari Surprise:
Share an unexpected and beautiful encounter.

_____

_____

"Hear the whispers of nature, and you'll find your path."

BEYOND THESE PAGES

A Deeper Dive into Art and Soul Awaits!

This book is but a chapter in a voyage where creativity meets depth.

Craving more? Explore the link below and weave deeper into the tapestry of art and emotion.

www.SFNonfictionBooks.com/Adult-Coloring-Books

A HEARTFELT THANK YOU

As the colors on these pages have come to life, so has our shared journey in this artistic realm. I am deeply grateful for your trust in choosing this book, and more so for allowing it to be a part of your self-care and personal journey.

Taking time for oneself is a gift—a silent promise of growth, introspection, and rejuvenation. By picking up the colors and filling these pages, you've not just created art but have also woven moments of peace, reflection, and creativity into your life.

Thank you for making space for yourself, for embracing the wonders within these pages, and for dancing to the rhythm of the lines and hues within this book. Your journey here is a testament to the beauty of dedicating time to one's soul and spirit.

If you enjoyed this journey and wish to explore more, know that there are other themes awaiting your artistic touch. Dive into new worlds and let your imagination flow.

From the deepest corner of my heart, thank you for bringing this book to life. Until our next artistic adventure together, cherish the colors of your journey and continue to shine.

Warmly,

Aventuras De Viaje

ABOUT THE AUTHOR

Aventuras has three passions: travel, writing, and learning new skills.

Combining these three things, Miss Viaje spends her time exploring the world and learning about anything and everything that interests her, from yoga, to music, to science, and more.

Aventuras takes what she discovers and shares it through her books.

www.SFNonfictionBooks.com

www.ingramcontent.com/pod-product-compliance
Lightning Source LLC
Chambersburg PA
CBHW081725100526
44591CB00016B/2508